Land, Love, Century

Land, Love, Century

New and Selected Poems by
Gevorg Emin

Translated by
Martin Robbins
with Tatul Sonentz-Papazian

With a Foreword by
Yevgeny Yevtushenko

An Original from Three Continents Press

©1988 Martin Robbins

First English-language Edition

Three Continents Press
1636 Connecticut Ave. N.W.
Washington, D.C. 20009

Library of Congress Cataloging-in-Publication Data:

Emin, Gevorg, 1919–
   Land, love, century.

      Translation of: Dar, hogh, ser.
      I. Robbins, Martin. II. Sonentz-Papazian, Tatul
III. Title.
PK8548.E5D313 1988   891'.99215   88-2218
ISBN 0-89410-625-2
ISBN 0-89410-626-0 (pbk.)

Cover art by Tatul Sonentz-Papazian
©1988 Three Continents Press
The cover design is of a *vishap,*
or old Armenian dragon; this motif is also
found in Armenian architecture and rugs.

Acknowledgments

Several members of the Armenian community helped in immeasurable ways to bring this book to publication. More than gratitude is due to Leo Hamalian for his encouragement, editorial and personal, in working on the translations over the years. Much appreciation is also due to Edmond Azadian for his help in the early stages of the project and to the Manoogian Fund for its support in preparing the manuscript. Thanks are also due to Richard McOmber, Director of the Armenian General Benevolent Union, for help in a crucial stage of the project. Finally, we would like to acknowledge the timely and important help of three other individuals and the organizations which they are part of: Manoog Young, Chairman, Board of Directors, National Association for Armenian Studies and Research; Syruan Palvetzian, Acting Executive Director, Diocese of the Armenian Church of America; and Louise Simone, through the Louise Simone Fund of the A.G.B U. for the generous support of the publication.

We would also like to credit the following publications for material in this book which appeared previously:

Ararat for Yevgeny Yevtushenko's introduction, "Mastery of the Spiritual," and for several of the translations which appeared in the Fall, 1987, issue. Several other translations appeared in

International Poetry Review, Nantucket Review, Poetry Now, Prism International, Sanscrit, Stone Country, and *Webster Review,* which we would like to acknowledge.

Table of Contents

LOVE

CENTURY

Foreword

"The Mastery of the Spiritual."

When I was in Yerevan and visited the Matenadaran, the treasure house of ancient manuscripts, I saw those Armenian manuscripts miraculously saved from the conquerors, kept in the cells of monasteries and caves. And I thought of the fate of the Armenian people.

The Armenian people had suffered too much. But they had succeeded in safeguarding and bringing their culture to us through the storms of centuries, like a candle protected by the palm of a hand.

Gevorg Emin is one of those protecting that candle. Whenever I think of Emin, I think of Armenian history. The nobility of a people is not determined by their numbers but by their spiritual wealth, their alertness of mind, their human and historical courage.

Emin's poems reflect the best of the Armenian working people and intellectuals. Their qualities of spiritual nobility include modesty, respect for others, and the discreet expression of feelings.

I met Gevorg Emin in the United States and can testify to his calm and immense dignity. He spoke to the Americans from the power and truthfulness of his spirit in representing Armenia and its culture to them.

Emin's mastery lies not only in the smoothness of his lines, but also in a spiritual mastery, a mastery of passionate conviction. Immensely interested in everything he comes into contact with, Emin might seem gloomy, but he's never bored.

This enormous curiosity and eagerness for life and the world is felt in all of Emin's poems. A curious man cannot be indifferent. This explains the kindness Emin shows toward everything that is bright and virtuous—and the hatred and scorn with which he rejects everything that hinders life.

Emin's poetry is full of wisdom and at the same time avoids the rationalistic-didactic emphasis which weighs heavily on most of our talented poets. In Emin's wisdom there is a playful inwardness that the reader immediately feels.

But the essense of Emin's spirit is the warmth of feeling toward the history and fate of the whole of mankind. Where does this come from? From the very fact that Emin loves his homeland, his soil, so passionately and deeply. His love for mankind begins with his love for his own Armenia. Without forcing his words, Gevorg Emin speaks as the devoted son not only of Armenia, but also of the whole world.

Yevgeny Yevtushenko
Moscow

Introduction

Gevorg Emin was born as Karlen Muradian in 1919 in Ash-
tarak, "a big village in the heart of Armenia." Commenting on
how folklore and locale shaped his poetry, he acknowledged the
influence of "the naive yet pithy tales of old men and the songs of
brides and young goodwives . . . . All that's best in me . . . and
my books was picked up . . . playing in the dusty Ashtarak streets
. . . near St. Mary's church . . . by the river Kassakh."

In 1927, his family left Ashtarak and moved to Yerevan, the
capital of Soviet Armenia. In 1936, he finished secondary school
and in 1940 graduated from the local Polytechnical Institute as a
hydraulic engineer. While in school, he met Armenia's leading
poet, Yegishe Charentz, and "became his son in poetry."

Charentz, who was killed during the Stalinist purges in 1937,
reshaped the young man's course. Charentz's poetry was influ-
enced by Mayakovsky and Pasternak. Most likely through
Charentz's mentorship, in 1936 Emin received an inscribed
copy of Pasternak's translation of *Hamlet,* which began a long
and important friendship.

The young Emin did work as a hydraulic engineer and de-
signed a power plant in the region of Vartenis. He talked of its
construction with characteristic modesty. I learned of it, through

an interpreter, when I first met Emin in 1972 (while he was touring the United States with Yevgeny Yevtushenko). I must have looked impressed because Emin quipped, in heavily accented English: "It's not Grand Coulee."

But the plant is still illuminating Armenia's heartland. Perhaps Emin saw the contrast between his power station and the new atomic plants when he wrote: "It's good to know that you're still radioactive, / A high tension powerline, a multi-digital number," in the poem "It's Good to Know," which begins this book's third section, "Century."

Emin's discipline as an engineer is important to his work. "Nothing like the exact sciences can help an author develop a sense of structural harmony, to avoid verbosity and dispense with the luxury of taking ten steps where one is sufficient," he wrote.

Yet another influence shaped Emin's poetry. In 1940, while still a student, he worked in the great depository of Armenian manuscripts, the Matenadaran. Medieval Armenia poetry "directly influenced" his writing. In the 1950s and 1960s his work "went back to free verse, which was the essential and only way poetry was written in the Middle Ages in Armenia," Emin revealed.

Then came the Second World War. Emin doesn't deal directly with it in this book. But in "Often I Cringe from a Shooting Pain," in the second section, "Love," Emin writes of the wound where "your deceitful love fed, / Love that I cut out with my own hand." Then he remembers "That's how a soldier gets a twinge . . . the curling of the fingers of that hand / which had been blown off some years ago."

The war shaped Emin's outlook in a broader way. He wrote that: "My generation has seen many difficulties since the best decades of our lives—years of war and difficult years of aftermath. And since at the proper time we haven't lived and loved as we should have, ours is a postponed generation."

Emin writes of his "postponed generation" with poignancy as he does in the love poem, "Longing": "Are you waiting as you used to wait for me? / Face stuck to the window's frosted square?" But the "gold" of his "emotions has not yet turned to lead"; he still has "ideals . . . the soulless stone of indifference / Is still distant and foreign to you," as he concludes "It's Good to Know."

It is good to know this poet whose concerns are much closer to us than the map with its imposed borders might indicate. The locale of the poems may be distant, but their language echoes universal concerns. In some ways, Gevorg Emin's poetry is like Robert Frost's. Both write of a rural locale and both use everyday speech. What appears to be nature poetry is not simply romantic but is modern and often harsh.

The Armenian genocide imposed still another dimension onto Emin's poetry. "To be silent about the crimes committed around us and to go on producing a so-called 'beautiful' literature is tantamount to being an accessory to those events," Emin commented.

Emin was never silent about a century where "nations and lands / With rowdy hollering split in two teams / And play football /. With this globe." As he wrote in "Over Ancient Manuscripts," he is a "Lover of light, sworn enemy of gloom / I lie and fight with phantoms in my room." He fights with both wit and wisdom, with wryness and wistfulness. He will not give in to the "lie [that] had mastered the microphone"; he insists on his "cry of human protest." But his "cry" can be subtle. In a poem about a statue of Stalin being taken down, he wrote that "no longer will boots be talking to heads."

Emin's work speaks to both our heads and our hearts. Responding to the modern poet's dismay with press and propaganda debasement of language, he asks in "Meditation" if there is "a bigger, more awful / Comedy, or tragedy, than to be a poet / And to believe that words and speech / Aren't worth an old penny in this world?" Emin may have wished "to be born mute, serene," as he concludes his "Meditation."

Gevorg Emin has spoken—through the rocks and grave-stones, the rivers and forests—of Armenia's predicament. But this wouldn't have gained international interest in his work, or won him a Soviet State Prize for *Land, Love, Century* (in 1976). His work speaks out of and to the deeper human predicament in the century of "Auschwitzes and Der Zors." In a century that is "pounding the skulls of the just," he asks: "Lord, don't you hear the red news of massacre and blood?"

But his poetry isn't full of shrillness or slogans. Emin's work is rooted in a past "bitter yet sweet . . . . Heady as hope, and sweet as faith / It flows." The flow of these poems, from the emerald green of Ashtarak to the streets of New York and Boston, lets us "read the life around" Gevorg Emin. This is essentially the life around ourselves, as Emin talks to our heads and our hearts in ways that, to use Richard II's words, make "a strange brooch of love in this all-hating world."

Martin Robbins
Boston

Land

ՄԵՆՔ

Եւ ի՞նչ էինք մենք
Ու երկիրը մեր,
Եթէ ծուռ նստենք, բայց խօսենք շիտա՛կ.-
Եթէ նաւ՝ապա չոր ժայռի վրայ,
Եթէ գաւ՝ ապա արցունքով լեցուն,
Եթէ հող՝ ապա քարացած ահից,
Եթէ քար՝ ապա ճչացող ցաւից,
Հզօր մի յոգի, որ չունէր մարմին,
Եզակի որակ՝ առանց քանակի,
Քաջարի սպայ, առանց բանակի,
Պաշտամունք՝ հնի ու աւերակի...

Եւ ի՞նչ էինք մենք
Ու երկիրը մեր,
Թէ շիտակ նստած՝ ծուռ խօսենք անգամ,-
Զրոսաշրջի՛կ իր հայրենիքում,
Հիւր՝ իր սեփական օճախ ու յարկում,
Անժողովուրդ հող,
Անհող ժողովուրդ
Եւ ցրուած հոլունիք, որ չեր ժողովում...

We

Yet what are we, think,
We and our country,
If our talk is frank, but we look away?
If we're a ship, we're aground on barren rock,
If we're clay we're filled with tears,
If we're soil we're petrified by fear,
And if we're stone—we cry out in pain,
A powerful soul with no body,
A rare quality without quantity,
A brave officer with no army,
A worshipper of the past and its ruin.

Yet what are we, think,
We and our country,
If our talk is frank but we look away?
We're tourists while at home,
Guests in our own houses,
A land without a people,
A people without a land,
Scattered beads, impossible to collect.

Ballad of the Home

1.

He couldn't remember his father's home—
Men come to this world born as men,
But as if marked with sin,
He came to the world . . . a refugee.

He couldn't remember his father's home—
When in Alexandretta, the hammer
In his hand to build a house, his own,
Said his mother:
              "My son, don't torture yourself
Placing stone on hard stone in vain,
All you need is a shack to get by,
It's all the same,
Sooner or later you'll go away . . ."

His mother was killed, her words survived;
The Turks had reached Alexandretta,
And surrendering the half-built house
To the catastrophe, he left for Lebanon.

2.

He couldn't remember his father's home—
But after he became a father,
In Beirut one day he picked up the hammer
To build a house, his own.
His wife this time:
              "In vain you make solid walls,

Dig deep foundations, adorn the pillars;
Don't take the foreigners' land as yours,
Sooner or later you'll go away . . ."

The poor woman died, her words survived;
Then welcome news of the return arrived,
And leaving the half-built house behind
He went back to his father's land.

3.

He couldn't remember his father's home—
Already feeble, shaky and old,
When in Yerevan he picked up the hammer
To build his house, his own,
Death said to him:
                    "Old man, heavy with sin,
What more do you want from this fleeting life?
Who cuts stone and mixes mortar
With one foot already in the grave?"

4.

Already the old man was painting
The roof, and in front of the new home
On the slopes of Ararat,
Stammering his first Armenian letters, the grandson.

At the Ashtarak Cemetery

When I'm wearied and worn down
By living for this hard land,
By pouring out tears for this land,
By writing songs for this land,
I come and sit on this stone,
Or in the shadow beneath this stone,
And, as in the past,
I look from this road and its dust
To the emerald flow of those orchards
To my Ashtarak,
My small old home,
A sky pierced by St. Mary's dome,
To my ancestors' still tombstones,
To Kassakh, my river, which flows
From the rocks of its steep ravines
And tells me again of this land
And those lives that passed
Through this transient world
On this soil they loved so much
That their heads lie on it still.

In the Forest

A little bird perched on a tree
Gives me free voice lessons,
Earth teaches me patience,
The bee, diligence unobserved,
And roots to grip the mother soil.

Rivulets and brooks
From each valley exhort me
To do kindness like one water-drop.
The mountain forces me
To keep my head up, proud,
The butterfly whispers to me,
Be content with even one day's life,
While the huge, far-off poplar advises me
That if I have to die,
Only to die erect.

And without difficulty, without torture . . .
Not like a human who in terror of death
Runs head-on into walls;
But to die like a tree, like a stone—
Serene, proud, and with dignity.

Landscape

I am this stone.
I am this rock.

I've only been on this earth two days,
But I've seen so much sorrow and betrayal,
Am so petrified with suffering and pain
That I'm already half stone and half man.
And if my time on earth would last,
Like stone I would be harder than stone.

I am this stone,
I am this tree.

Haven't I, like it,
Given of myself
Fruit to this land,
And shade to all who pass by,
And haven't they
Broken my branches,
Hacked at my trunk,
Certainly knowing
No matter what they do,
Gripping with my roots
Into this unforgiving land,
I shall give them
My fruit and harvest,
My gold of autumn,
the lamb of my spring.

I am this tree.

And I Understood

And I understood
Just now understood
(When my own hopes
Were thrown down, broken)
Why all the people
Who raise their hands in prayer
Will hold both hands above their heads.

Suffering, hopeless
In their dread . . . terror . . .
It seems to them
The sky up there threatens
To cave in on their vulnerable heads,
The old and young . . .

And they raise high
Their shaking hands
To ward off their death,
Somehow to survive.

Little

We're little, oh yes,
Little
As pebbles that career down a mountain
And gain strength like a boulder in a field

Little
Like our mountain torrents
Which store up enormous power
Not heard
In the still curl of a valley stream

We're little, oh yes,
Yet who has told you
To press us with such pain
That our duress turns us into diamonds

And who forced you
To scatter us like stars everywhere
So you keep seeing us
Wherever you go.

We're little
But we're like our native land
Whose borders reach out from
Byurakan's telescopes to the moon
And from Lousavan back to ancient Urartu.

Little
Like the miracle of uranium,
Which shines century after century,

Radiates
A glow
Which is not consumed.

First Snow

I'm not griping, don't get me wrong;
So there's no snow and winter's come along.
I'd only like to ask one question:
Concerning our spring . . . when did it happen?
And when did it pass through mountains and valleys?
So that . . . again winter's here—so suddenly.

Long-Awaited Spring

Trees, this year it's a false spring, listen.
After the long, unending freeze
Now the heat of an hour's thaw
And you've gone crazy—wait.

Don't open this year's buds yet.
Spring isn't here.
Hard winter still lies in ambush
To trick you—it only looks like spring.

You're not yet ice,
You've still to freeze,
Tighten your buds even
Tighter, fist-like.

Stand up to this spring's
False front—
In the name of the coming
Long-awaited spring.

Winter Scene

I told him a thousand times
That crazy painter autumn:
"It's a shame to waste your paints,
It's silly to pour it on thick
And squander the colors you've got—
This red paint here
This yellow one there
And that gray one . . ."

But he got all worked up
And paid no attention.
So now from a thousand shades
Just one color remains
Just that white one there
Which he's smearing
(Needed or not)
Wherever it may fall—

Over stone
A roof
Vineyard or mountain . . .

Painting a boring winter.

Smart Lamb

The smart lamb feeds off of two mothers
—Folk saying

Lamb, smart lamb
Who feeds off of two mothers,
Why are you knocking yourself out,
Stooping so low
When you're going to end up
As a sheep anyhow?

Dialogue

A dangerous nothingness
Has infested our house—
Like bedbugs sucking
Blood—its bite stings.

You're a man, correct?
And it's just an insect,
So why not move your index finger
In a little massacre
And kill it?

Friend, haven't you ever killed a bedbug?
It smells far worse when you squash it
Than its pitiful bite or poison.

16

Firefly

Oh, firefly, you stupid bug,
Who told you, stubborn, relentless,
To give off light alone there
In the darkness—a glow which warmed
Everyone, but sad to say
Gave away your position.

If you gave off no light,
Who could have spotted you, to cut
Your life's short thread
And throw you down, crushed.

In this night's doubled black,
I suffer for you—and what you did.

Luckless Butterfly

Whose life lasts for just one day
And who takes wings in this world
On a rainy day.

Luckless traveler,
Armenian pilgrim who for just one week
From the end of the world
Will land within sight of Mt. Ararat
And that very same week
All of Armenia is covered with clouds
From Massis to Sevan.

Luckless generation
whose life is only
half of a century
and is born in this world,
in this atomic dark age.

Luckless is he
who has understood this,
and lucky the one
who does not understand.

The Owl

Years ago somehow the owl sinned
And it's ashamed of the light.
All night the owl suffers, the owl
Sighs and begs, cries out to me,
And I suffer through a sleepless night.

What can I do? Stay up so I too
Hear everything? Should I learn to feel
His suffering, soothe his sorrow, disperse
His doubts? Write so the whole world hears of it?
My god, isn't my own lot enough!

The owl sighs, the owl begs.
For that and because of the owl itself
I suffer and stay up, sleepless.

So what can I do? Whose sorrows should I
Listen to? Whose sins banish with my songs?
Me, supersensitive and thus unhappy,
Abandoned instead of having the friendship
Of women, or of men, treated like a convict.

What can I do, I was born a poet?
I am a man, too.
But only one man.

Horses

Horses,
How harmonious you are,
How natural
        . . . and how human.
How much more sensible
Than me and this girl,
Who, poor thing,
Is torturing me
And herself.

You stand out in the fields,
Face to face,
You nuzzle into each other's mane,
You gaze at the world and each other
With huge
Dewy
And sage eyes,
And you make no sound,
Don't say a word—
You neither define love
Nor embitter an already bitter leave taking

With elegant contempt
Or crude banter
Or a long and dragged-out settlement.

How jealous I am of you,
Horses.

The Piano

It had begun to seem like a chest already,
To seem like an old and dusty chest;
The fat little owner had locked it firmly
And stashed the key deep in his vest,
And lined up seven white elephants on top,
Two thick albums,

                 and one cupid (plaster-cast).
It had started to look like a chest already,
Which once long ago had been a piano.

Oppressive and hot, the room was smokey with the racket
From banging backgammon that brought down some plaster;
While under those elephants, haughty and white,
Like flowers wasting under rocks,
Were trapped a sonata by Bach,
"Andouni" by Komitas (which mourned for him),
Chopin waltzes dampered by fear,
And the outcry of a deaf Beethoven.

The dolma was gobbled down,

                 to that backgammon rattle,
The beer flowed over, heads splitting foam;
The "Chief Engineer" beamed down from cloud nine—
The table sagged,

              Ararat through the window.
And finally, when onto that greasy floor
Somebody stomped with drunken yelling,
The piano strings began a muted jangling
Like a long pent sigh from its neglected corner.

Then my heart rebelled against all time that is shut;
And my fingers, prying, finally forced the lid open
And caressed into sound the singing keys
(Half blackened by sorrow,
                                    half frozen white by fear);
I shook the piano's solid black shoulder,
While seven white elephants sailed toward the floor—
With the unemployed cupid (already smashed).

And then the chest became a piano.
Had anyone tried to caress it ever?
Had anyone listened to its mute soul,
Which yearned to fulfill its mission forever?
Overcome by a storm, it laughed through its tears,
Spoke of sorrows locked tight for years . . .
"All of a sudden our poet is drunk . . ."
"Nah, he just knocked all those elephants down . . ."

The piano was locked by stubby fingers,
The fat little owner turned back to his cronies;
He'd never known how to make any music—
So nobody else would tickle those ivories.

As I hunched home, cold wind cut me,
And my heart coached me for a performance—
So what if a chubby cupid would mock me,
And seven elephants gawk from where they crashed.

Don't weep, piano, don't—you hear me?
I'll take you out of that alien house.

The Prayer of an Armenian Poet

"Who is to blame for this murderous idea?
To put—of all the places in the world,
Ararat the white,
Ararat the unspotted,
In a place where for years,
Centuries it would bleed
Even to its tip.

"Who thought it up?
To make a hell
Where Eden was, or wasn't,
In Mt. Ararat's shade.
Instead of earth, dry stones,
Instead of water, blood.

"Who thought it up?
Even at our history's first light
To place the head of this life-giving
Ancient people under
A neighbor's bloody sword,
Demanding he sell his soul
If he chooses to save his body.

"And if the past centuries
Haven't yet been able to save him,
And if the coming ones
Won't be able to save him,
And an improbable miracle
Is the only probable answer—

"Lord, give me, like the prophet Moses,
The power to uproot and remove
My persecuted race
From this place, Armenia—
No, this place of death,
No, this place of rocks—
To another safe shore
(Is there such a place?)
My indestructible race,
Its new seed with ancient roots
Of story, song, and monument.

"Give to this wordmaker
His magic impediment,
And his rod to split
Rocks until they gush water,
And his staff to divide
The red sea of our luck
(Our tears and our blood),
Even if, like the prophet Moses,
I find my death and am buried
In alien earth before
Reaching the promised shore
At the beloved threshold of its closed door.

"Lord, don't you hear
The red news of massacre and blood?"

Love

Longing

Longing, shapeless as this cloud,
Drifted through my heart,
Touching its chambers with dampness;—

What are you up to
Right now in this cold evening hour?
Are you at home or out,
Proud or humble?
Are you waiting as you used to wait for me?
Face stuck to the window's frosted square?
And does this rain seem to trace
The glass like tears?

Or you love no more
But you just can't walk away yet,
And the longing just like this shapeless cloud
Has found you as well,
And your heart is wet,
Damp with sadness.

Dialogue

I walked into the woods with a buddy.
Everything there seemed so different:
Flower,
      tree,
            gleam of sunrise.
"God that's beautiful," I said.
"No big deal," he said, off-hand.
"Big deal or not, I'm in love again."

Come On, Tonight Let's Have Fun—

Set the table,
My nymphet, my snare,
My twinge of remorse.
Let's lay upon the table
The tender shoot of your dalliance,
The ripe fruit of my torment,
The lavish tray of your spell,
My temptation's bitter voice,
The new wine of your passion,
The blood-red pomegranate of my desire.
Let's have some fun.

Often I Cringe From a Shooting Pain

Why does it hurt me?
What hurts me?
In panic, I look and I look,
I feel it, and I'm unaware that I fear
That what hurts me is that wound
Where your deceitful love fed,
Love that I cut out with my own hand
In search of release, desperate with pain.

That's how a soldier gets a twinge—
Simple, palpable, without a doubt
The curling of the fingers of that hand
Which had been blown off some years ago.

Say "Good Morning" to the Old Ones,

They're halfway into the dark already
And rejoice every morning
That they've struggled up from the dark again.

Ask them, "How did the night pass?"
They themselves are half night already
And are lucky each morning
That today, again, thank god, they woke up.

Don't anger the old ones,
They're half-filled with anger already;
They've wrestled all night with Death's angel
And are happy that, again, they've won.

And don't add burdens to their old shoulders;
For them the burden of age is enough.

Your Hands

I love your hands
Which for so many years now
Hold me but never
Capture me,

Make me the master of the world
But never master me.

They encircle, but don't
Choke, only save me
The way that drowning
Men are saved.

Your loving hands,
So magical
And melodic.

In their palms,
I, a dry shell,
Little by little
Become a pearl.

I love your hands.

And Whoever You Might Be

. . . And whoever you might be in this world,
Even the whore whom everyone hates,
When . . . you love, when you're inspired, or . . . pregnant,
You become the Mother of God—or God.

You become as clean as the dirt or manure
From which flowers bloom and is no more
Lowly dirt or manure but . . . "holy, holy,"
"Ave," "Glory to God," "Alleluia."

. . . Seeing a woman pregnant touches me,
I warm to her, I admire
The unrelenting apprehension
With which she sees deep into herself

And hears what, sadly, we can't hear,
Smiling to the one smiling within,
Tearful when there's crying within,
And is shaken by the concealed one's movements . . .

Like the seven dolls of an old Russian toy,
Inside each one still a doll one smaller—
She carries her baby inside her
And the one the baby will bear.

I love her crying without any reason,
Fear of the unseen, stir of unknown feelings
And the goodness, the pure goodness
Of those gods with two hearts.

Sing a Song for Me

Sing a song for me
But sing it in a style
Which doesn't have any beginnings
Or endings of phrases.
Touch me with it
In a way that costs me nothing
Like this quiet rain
Which is just for me
Yet for everyone.

Sing a song for me
But sing it in a style
Which doesn't deal at all with cause
And effect,
With receivables
Or with payables.

So sing a song for me,
But don't sing about
What has happened
And nothing about
What exists now,
Not even what will be,

But something else,
About something different
Which is neither past
Nor present, priceless,
Not even future,
Bright or obscure.

Why do you hold back?
Sing for me.

Final Song

I don't know whether I'm losing
Or finding something;
But whatever they ask me,
I smile sadly.

Do they cheer wildly in faith?
I smile sadly.
Do they flee, horrified, from fanatics?
I smile sadly.

I smile sadly,
Look at victim and killer,
Hearing words empty and wise,
Look to the newborn,
To those new-buried.

Has old age caught up with me?
Or am I finding myself?
But is it worth thinking about?
I smile sadly.

Song of the Poet

I know
The saints are all out of date,
All the new temples
Built today are old before
Their paint dries,
And the only new things
Call us with sin's voice.
All the sacred books are old,
All the bells that call us to prayer,
And the only new thing
Is my life, sadly fading.

And Man's mind,
Though it can control
Even the sun's force,
His heart still
Grunts like a homonid.

The poet is the mad lover
Of this terrible age . . .
The momentary simple husband,
The favorite servant.

I swear that even tomorrow's
Le Monde is already old
And the real news
Is the "Song of Songs."

Writer's Block

For two months
I have not written
A word.

My voice, a low
Grumble, disturbs
Our quarter

Like the rumble
Of a millstone
Which, having nothing to grind,
Grinds itself.

Only Yesterday

Just yesterday,
My whole life
Was just ahead of me;
All time was mine.
And so what?
What could I do with it?
Where could I go,
When I saw no roads open?

And now, countless
Roads unending
Open wide
Ahead of me,
Beckon. But what
Can I do? Where
Can I go, when
My life's behind me

And time has hit the road.

By This Age

All the geniuses were long in their graves,
They died fighting at their posts,
Victims of a plot or a king,
Thrown down into dark and mute cells,
Lying back on the laurels of their glory;
Or they discovered
That they couldn't take one free breath
To be inspired and inspire.
So they erased their lives like a misplaced line.

At this age,
Whoever is still alive,
If he had been a Don Juan
Has already become a husband,
If he'd been an inspired actor
Would already be a producer,
If he'd been a young champion
Would be just another trainer,
And the writer works on his memoirs
When everything has turned to memory.

At this age,
In this bad time,
He alone can keep his youth
Who held his convictions high,
Who applied his colors pure,
Whose inspiration
Was natural as breathing—
The way that light shines,
The way a young tree shudders—

He whose deep hungers
Have no measure, number, equation,
Beyond good,
Beyond evil,
When age doesn't matter anymore.

Dream

I dreamed I was dead,
Laid out in my coffin.
Someone had crossed my arms
And the candle branded my heels.
I was just plain dead.
Well, goddammit,
Who's immortal?
Yet my dream oppressed me so
I wouldn't wish it on an enemy.

So I saw I was dead.
Around me, alive and happy,
Someone kisses his beloved,
Another reads a book.
From a walnut in bloom
A lark praises spring.

The waters of Zangu murmur,
A girl waters a lawn,
A child studies words,
The poet writes a new song,
And you'd think nothing's changed
By the fact that I
No longer exist.

The world goes on its way
And, you'd think, notices nothing.
Have you had such bad dreams?
Maybe you don't care,
But I twitched, as if I were hit,

In the middle of this damned dream.

To die?
That's understandable,
It's the order of things;
But to live and breathe in this world
And not to feel
That you're important to life,
Compared to that, what is death?

What good's this life on earth
If I can't feel
That the world's my home,
That I too build walls
And change ancient riverbeds,
That life sings my song
While I take my words from life,
That I've built new roads
And have even set the sun on fire.

I know it's just a dream,
But, whether I'm dead or alive,
There it is,
My bet and the dream's
Are the same:
Yet it will never happen.

What is Death?

When bread and wine
Bless my table,
And I'm in love
And writing poems?

It is that real bread
Whose seeds die in the soil,
But through their death
Become new bread.

It's the juice of those grapes
Buried in the soil each autumn,
But, reborn each spring
Come to life again.

It is the love that sometimes
Is even harder than death,
And is the only love
That conquers the dreaded dungeon.

And it is that verse,
Which by denying death
Perpetuates this living moment.

So, what is death?
And even if it comes,
It can't take these things I have.

And Who Is the Poet

And who is the poet, and what is his work?
At the cost of suffering,
Being bereaved of things you don't have,
Often at the cost
Of a whole life's ransom,
To create a good line, one metaphor
(That feels new in your own hands)
Only to learn the next day
With regret that it, too,
(As everything under this moon)
Was on a known
And ancient page
Written in Nero's days,
A truth of science,
And then was lost
In the dust of an old attempt.
Oh, the poet's torturous vocation.

Meditation

The simpler you speak what you mean to say,
The more they misunderstand what you say.
And what good is this damned tongue
If the world misunderstands anyway?

The more the true word is repeated,
The steeper the chasm of mistaken speech
Deepens. Is there a bigger, more awful
Comedy, or tragedy, than to be a poet
And not to believe that words and speech
Aren't worth an old penny in this world?

Whatever tongue you write in, or scream in,
Isn't it the same whichever tongue
They don't understand you in? And what to do?
Withdraw, shut your lips, your windows, your house?

Oh unquenchable yearning
To become mute,
To be born mute, serene.

Doesn't It Seem to You,

Haven't you wondered
When a shooting star showers
The ground with shards,
When a meteorite's fragments
Fall to earth,
Hasn't it seemed to you
That from far-away planets
It's the remnants of star-ships
Flying toward us,
Burning in heaven
As they drift to our globe?

And now, when our rockets burn
And scatter down on alien globes
Do they know it out there?
That these flamed-out stars
Are fragments of our smoldering ships,

Or do they call them fallen shooting stars,
And write songs, or
Maybe . . . make a wish?

Century

It's Good to Know

It's good to know that you're still radio-active,
A high tension powerline, a multi-digital number,

That you belong not just to yourself but you're everywhere.
That to some you're like light, to others a magnet or fire,

That the impossible gives you wings,
That you're also a spring or a taut wire.

That the gold of your emotions has not yet turned to lead,
That you still have ideals, you have goals and a course,

That in daytime you live in warm passions,
At night your life is ruled by women's whims,

And that the soulless stone of indifference
Is still distant and foreign to you.

Twentieth Century

Twentieth century:
So I thought I'd already grown up
And was quite a man
Had read Goethe
And heard Beethoven,
Stammered Hegel;
All over again
I'd become a brat,
Battering this century
Like a toy,
Splitting the world in halves.

Twentieth century:
I who became light's inventor,
And fire
While in the cave still,
Reaching skyscrapers from those walls,
Now obscuring the light I labored over,
I entered the cave once again,
Fearing myself
And the threat of the atom my hands have split.

Twentieth century:
Oh neon light,
Or Nero's light,
Which gives us the jitters
With the Gestapo's and Der Zors' dark terrors,
In comparison
The middle ages have melted down
Our recollection like its black candles;

Where nations and lands
With rowdy hollering split in two teams
And play football
With this globe,
With this earthen ball.

Twentieth century:
Praise for the legs of Brigitte Bardot;
Bedside vigil for a cancer-killed man
With the insane wails of jazz;
And doing the twist
On the fresh graves of loved ones.

Twentieth century:
With its thinking machines,
With its robot-like men
Who from Der Zors to Oscwiecm
Have been drinking blood;

Indictment
Written into the Bible's clean margin;
The worship of the hips
And the mind taboo.

Twentieth century:
With its nerves tightly wound,
Its liver filled with bile
And blood-congealed heart;
When death has now come
From everything
Which gave rise to being,
Rain,

The wind,
And the light's beam.

Twentieth century:
You dash out the brains of the just
And guzzle whiskey as you hug the hangman;

The press trades in lies,
The truth is strung up
On the radio's transmitter towers,
And is crucified
On all the TV antennas.

Twentieth century:
Nations enslaved have been freed,
Those which were free are newly enslaved;
And for all of the old life enigmas
Precision's clues conjure up
More complex questions.

Twentieth century:
The human mind and its light divine,
Lampshades made out of human skin;
The scribbles of modern painting apeing
The old cave dwellers,
Words severed from thought,
How long will they push you down twisted paths?

Twentieth century:
Atomic mushroom
On the cradle of a new born child,
And atomic rain

On the funerals of the old;
Will you be the last,
Twentieth century,
Smashed by atoms?
Or will you continue
Into the Twenty First,
The century to follow?

No, they can't take you back to the middle ages
And they can't call you by tyrants' names,
You'll become the century
Of truth
Of good
And the just.

You witness this conflict, this proof of hard progress,
And I, your poet . . . of the middle ages.

Ave Maria

Ave Maria . . .
With skeleton hands
Of Auschwitz and Der Zor
Stretching toward you,
With napalm-seared eyes,
With Hiroshima's wounds
Never scarred over,
With torn-out tongue
And brain crushed

Let me sigh to you
Let me beg of you

It's enough, Maria . . .

No more
This rumble of roofs which have crumbled,
And minds which are numbed,
Evil most abundant,
When the fist is made by power,
The conscience is clear . . .
Ave Maria . . .

It's enough
All the bombs poised overhead,
Monasteries deserted,
The jails overcrowded,
Zeal of fanatics scorching the planet,
And the powerless books,
The powerless songs,

Are now as feeble
As all of the sighs,
All the entreaties
We dedicate to you . . .

Ave Maria . . .

. . . Do they get to you,
All of our prayers?
Or is our faith as well
Anointed with the oil
Of betrayal, Maria . . .

Ave Maria . . .

Garcia Lorca, Spain, 1936

The native land isn't just earth and water,
Neither, Spain, are hymns and orations;
No longer will I call you "Mother"
If you've become the mother of tyranny.

No longer will I give to Caesar
What belongs to God and heaven;
I'd rather be long forgotten
Than be a genius who's a jester.

No longer will I accept presents,
The gold showered on Danae was shame;
No longer will I be forced into silence.
If you are Franco . . .
                                    I am Don Quixote.

No longer will I argue with you in seriousness
If what props you up is vengeance and envy;
No longer will I roam in packs,
I wasn't born a wolf . . .
                                    a man stands alone.

No longer will I write or speak
When they've emptied truth from words;
No longer will I listen to you talk—
Even listening to you is collaboration.

No longer can I fight your tyranny,
I can't sink to fighting filth with filth;
No longer can I even breathe—

You've poisoned the air we breathe.

No longer can I live a time
Which can't tell wheat from chaff;
No longer will I cling to life
When they've condemned me to live.

Oh, how you tyrants cherish
The poet already turned to ashes.

So I'm putting a period after this life;
I don't want to see you auction my glory.

Yellow Press

Oh, poison tongue of the yellow press . . .
If you read tomorrow
In the sheet of some Herald
That you stole a star from heaven
(And they'll get witnesses),
Do not, in vain, deny it
And defend yourself;
The lie thrives on denials,
And each denial of a sin that never was,
Somehow, to some degree,
Accepts the guilt . . .

If they insist
That you were seen,
Or that in Paris
You sat on Bardot's lap
(Wish it were true),
Or that you robbed
The Chase Manhattan Bank;
Do not, in vain, deny it,
And don't resent it . . .

Under this sun,
One does only
What one can;
The dog barks,
The caravan passes . . .

In the New York Hospital

Life, how complex in its mystery.
The key?
So everyday, so simple.

Gentlemen,
You are tormenting yourselves, sleepless,
To discover if this or that man
Has cancer.

So murderous the surroundings of your world,
Men so unforgiving to men,
That when suddenly
One of you feels like
A sister, brother,
Close friend
All become tender
And considerate,
Good—

He has to be
Sick with cancer, there's no doubt,
And leaning over his bed—death.

Gravestone in a Negro Cemetery

Who can I convince, how,
(And is it worth it?)
That I, who knows,
Might have been
The world's best actor;
And what could I do,
An actor's life is just a day.
Our director,
Dull, no talent,
And the good parts
Got cast by fawning
Or paying off;
So they didn't see the stage,
The light alive in me
And buried with me—
Othello, Lear, and Hamlet
(As are buried in a closed piano
Bach's sonata and Gershwin's blues).
How to say it?
Who to convince
(And is it worth it?)
My talent and voice,
True gifts above
All the songs and voices
You ever heard;
But I was only heard
By Harlem's dirty alleys
And a broken-down hotel—
While the one with no voice
Walked all the glittering stages.

And how to say it,
To whom, and why?
That I really knew
The true word
That would save
This demented world;
But the lie had mastered the microphone,
And no one could hear
The cry of my human protest,
And the lie's leering whisper
Thundered through the whole world.

How to say it,
And to whom,
And why?
(Is it worth it?)
Men understand each other
As much as the dead
In this graveyard.

First Night in New York

In the beginning God created the jet plane—
And the universe was formless and void,
Though there was engine noise
From which the angels flew away,
Flapping their nylon wings
While God put on
A cosmonaut's helmet
So he wouldn't go deaf.

Then God created water—
Rivulet, branch,
Stream, river,
Lakes, sea, and ocean—
And there was water
On earth, much more
Than it's possible to squeeze
From all the false books,
Newspapers, and speeches.

Then the earth seemed water-logged
So God created land—
Country, island, peninsula,
Warm and cold continents—
Enslaved and free,
Yellow and white,
Red and black;
And, grabbing the microphone,
He said:
"Form battalions, armies,
Arm yourselves with mortars and rockets,

Fight each other,
Devastate and annihilate each other."

Then God looked down from heaven,
Bored by vistas of desert and wastelands,
And created New York.
It was fireworks!
An orgy of lights,
Jewelry stores with windows
That touched the heavens,
A feast, a blow out!

And God loved New York
Because even though he'd created it,
He'd never been in New York;
And when
Down lit-up stairs of a skyscraper
He descended from heaven to Broadway,
A black form
Stuck a knife into His side.

They crucified Him,
On TV antennas
Between two thugs—

Hallelujah
Hallelujah—

And on the cross
God sighed,
He pleaded:
"If possible, Lord,

Lord Gagarin,
Lord Shepard,
Lord Armstrong,
Take this Babylon away from me,
And take me to heaven,
The moon,
Or—hell."

In the Streets of Boston

It seems
All the Christs
Have descended from crosses
And not quite recovered,
Stagger,
Pale, near death,
Wandering on Boston sidewalks
Looking like hippies.

Shake their hands
And you touch each bleeding scar;
And on their sides
Under the tattered jeans
There are wounds—
From a lance?
Or a knife
During a fight?
Isn't it the same?

Strippers are dancing
In night clubs
And nobody watches;
Restaurants and bars
Burst with crowds of Christs
While the crosses are empty.

Magdalene, denounces prayers of repentant
Whores with each step,
And there is no Mary,
The Mother of God isn't there—

Maybe she's got cancer,
Maybe she choked to death
On the smoke of marijuana and hasheesh.

One Christ
Couldn't really have atoned
For so much sin.
And my voice,
Rough in my throat,
And the noise of the twist
Roars:
"Where are you?
Why aren't you being crucified,
New Christs?"

And, I don't know,
Is it the whiskey flowing,
Or it's the hippies
Who whisper in my ear:
"Christ had a father—
Unlike our fathers,
A wayward
Or Gestapo-tortured father,
But an omnipotent God;
Christ knew
No matter how he suffered,
Even crucifixion,
It's the same,
He'd be resurrected.

"What a Christ!
He was a star of a Jewish movie,

James Bond,
007 Super Agent.

"We are the Christ;
A generation
Come to this earth
For one week only,
The one week
When the world is Sodom and Gomorrah,
Babylon,
War, famine,
And nuclear blast.

"We are the Christ,
Who every day
And every step are crucified
And have no hope of resurrection,
No Father-God,
No Mother of God.

"We, whose torment
Is seven times heavier
And meaningless,
And meaningless.

"Should we go back onto the cross?
Aren't there enough crosses already—
Of denial, of alienation,
Of faith forever lost?

"And why? Why be crucified
When—look anywhere you want—

You'll find nothing around you
Worth being crucified for."

Night

Grave,
Huge,
Heavy black dreams
Like large prayer beads, bulging
On the thin, thin string of my sleep . . .

Good omen?
Bad?
God?
Who knows . . .

Someone to Answer

You answer
All your child's questions,
All the *why's.*

You wish there were
Someone to answer yours.

When you're boxed in,
You turn to God
With your prayers
And your pleas.

But He (if he's there),
Whom will He ask,
What will He do?

Smile, If You Like

Smile, if you like, your whole life,
If you like, be sad and cry,
Live plush, in a palace, if you like,
Or sweat for a piece of bread,
Take any road you pick,
Get old any way, anywhere you choose—
The same net of wrinkles will mark
My forehead, and yours, and his.
Who can glance at them and understand
Whose life was grief and whose a laugh?

Someone, it seems, neglected to write
Across our foreheads—or left it half-done—
The one word or name
Which could tag our luck.

At the Barber's

1.

As if it's a plot (all as one),
They torture me.
"Don't swing your legs"—
That's my father, already had his shave.
And the barber:
"Keep your head still, can't you?"
But the scissors tickle me
And falling hair
Prickles my knees.

Is it the sunbeam from the scissors on my face,
Or it's my gold curl again
Dancing on the mirror's lake?

It's sun!
It's spring!

2.

Red-haired, the plump lady barber
Shaves off my long-expected mustache,
Pulls at my tangled hair
So she can comb it.
Her warm thigh brushes my leg—
The whole world's a miracle to me.

"A hot towel?"
"Yes, please!"

"Shampoo?"
"Yes, please!"
"Dry it?"
"Yes, please!"

Do whatever you want,
And for shaving a non-existent mustache
I'm ready to pay
This goddess in a white smock
All my student's stipend—
And the whole world with it.

The spring shower outside
Is like my black, shining hair.

3.

Is it the day, or am I depressed?
I want to get smashed,
To curse and weep.
Like lightning at my temple
The scissors flash.
Crack! and black hairs fall.
Crack! and white ones
On the dirty floor.

Black rain outside,
White snow outside;
Winter that's yet to come,
And autumn passing.

4.

They're falling—
The white hair falls,
White mustache and beard.
White barber and smock,
And the mirror's surface
Seems to freeze.

Outside, snow
Sifts down like powder.
What's that music?
Who's being buried?

5.

I've heard that hair—
What is hair?—
Keeps on growing
(God save us)
After death.

"A compress? Shampoo?"
"For God's sake—leave it!"

Striptease

A tinselled girl sways
To the jazz beat
(*S'il vous plaît, Madame,*
What's your name?).
Is she singing,
Dancing or declaiming;
No,
She takes it off, piece by piece.

Oh, the man's eternal itch,
This single miracle right there on stage,
There in the spotlight, her thighs are flashing,
One more grind
And there! White miracles, her breasts.
There!
(Maybe you expected a figleaf
In this atom-smashed, brazen age.)
And Madame Eve, sensual, breathless,
Shivers, naked,
Twisting, sinuous.

Oh, the man's eternal itch,
But you, male, craving this instant,
Why aren't you enflamed by her heat?
Why are you frozen before this bare flesh
As one freezes before all naked things
Forced on you over and over again?

At the Night Club

Now, everything's the same to me.
Isn't it true that the most terrifying end
Is better than unending terrors?
Let it happen fast, whatever happens—
Waiter, more wine.

The victim's ashes
Already mix with the executioner's.
And all was dust and has become as dust.
Now, you can't tell the gasp of the strangled
From the grunt of the strangler—
Waiter, another.

There's no end to it all
And no beginning.
Shall we ever see the real end and ending?
And is there anyone who understands the past
And vigils over the future—
Straight up, waiter.

Is it already falling
Onto the sidewalks and on the rooftops
That poisonous atomic rain,
Drop by drop, which will fall upon our graves—
Waiter, a cocktail.

Bring brandy
And wine,
Cocktails and whiskey
And the noise of jazz,

Without end,
Without beginning.

Insomnia

Again I'm sleepless.

The rain water drips through this worn out roof,
Its sounds, missing the rusted pail,
Drip into my brain,
And my mind's driven
Toward a run down district
And sorrow that's muted
By this relentless drip.

This spring rain
Is poisoned, promises death
Not only in far off
Hiroshima
But on this sidewalk
And in this orchard.

I'm still sleepless.

Now sleep approaches my wide open eyes,
And flicked by the blink of my lashes, flees,
And before my eyes
While the newest rocket
Streaks toward the moon and on to Mars,
Oh how many people are sleepless,
How many hearts weighed down
And tongues made silent,
And how many eyes, in their pain stare out
Into the night's darkness and into my own eyes,
Screaming, wordless: "Man,

80

What are you doing?"
With each new rocket and each new spaceship
Headed further away
And even quicker—
But tell us where,
Where are you speeding to? . . .
So many sorrows
Under uncounted rooftops on this earth
And this rocket's newly discovered path
Leads us back to the cave of early man.

I'm still without sleep.

So many years ago
Grabbed by the Gestapo, accused of a crime,
And over the years
Exonerated only there in the grave
Many dead ones
Rise up
To resist,
Hunting down their executioners in vain.

I'm sleepless again.

And feverishly I hunt through my papers,
Write about all of this with words,
In the human tongue,
Which I doubt many understand anymore.

I'm still sleepless.

Do you hear, people,

Love,
Comrade,
Brother,
This terrible age?
Put me to sleep
Or wake up all those men
Whose sleep vainly promises
A hollow instant of forgetfulness.

Again I'm sleepless.

Biographical Sketches

Gevorg Emin is Armenia's foremost living poet. He won the Soviet State Prize with *Land, Love, Century.*

Tatul Sonentz-Papazian is a graphics designer, trained in Cairo and Europe. He is also in charge of Hairenik Publications, the oldest Armenian press in the United States.

Martin Robbins has published translations from German, Italian, and Spanish, as well as four books of his own work.